5|98
98

jB
KELLEY

Saller, Carol.

Florence Kelley.

$18.60

DATE			

BAKER & TAYLOR

Florence Kelley

by Carol Saller
illustrations by
Ken Green

Carolrhoda Books, Inc./Minneapolis

To Richard—C.S.
To my aunt, Wreathea Maxwell—K.G.

The photograph on page 48 appears courtesy
of the Library of Congress.

Text copyright © 1997 by Carol Saller
Illustrations copyright © 1997 by Ken Green

Carolrhoda Books, Inc., c/o The Lerner Publishing Group
241 First Avenue North, Minneapolis, MN 55401 U.S.A.

Library of Congress Cataloging-in-Publication Data

Saller, Carol.
    Florence Kelley / by Carol Saller ; illustrations by
Ken Green.
      p.   cm.—(A Carolrhoda on my own book)
    Summary: A biography of the determined woman who
worked to improve the lives of children, the poor, and
adult workers.
    ISBN 1-57505-016-1
    1. Kelley, Florence, 1859–1932—Juvenile literature.
2. Women social reformers—United States—
Biography—Juvenile literature. 3. Children—
Employment—United States—History—Juvenile l
iterature. [1. Kelley, Florence, 1859–1932. 2. Reformers.
3. Women—Biography.] I. Green, Ken, ill. II. Title.
III. Series.
HQ1413.K45S25 1996
303.48'4'092—dc20
    [B]   96–18300

Manufactured in the United States of America
1 2 3 4 5 6 – JR – 02 01 00 99 98 97

Introduction

There was a time, not so very long ago, when many American children went to work every day. They were not slave children. But for some of them, life was like slavery. Some children worked in factories from early morning until past dinnertime. Others worked in the fields all day, in the rain or in the hot sun, picking cotton or tobacco. Some worked 12 hours a day, 6 days a week. These children did not go to school. They had little time to play. They were often tired and sick. And some were as young as five years old.

How could this be? There are laws that say children cannot work. Other laws say they must go to school. In 1891, there were not many laws like that. But that year, a woman who lived in Chicago began to visit the homes and factories where poor people lived and worked. And she decided something had to be done. This woman was Florence Kelley.

When Florence Kelley was seven years old,
she read a book
about poor children in England.
These children did not go to school.
They couldn't play like Florence could.
They were poor and had to work.
The book showed pictures of
small children carrying loads of wet clay
on their heads. Florence thought
they looked like little trolls.
The book upset her.

Later, when Florence was 12,
her father took her to visit
a huge glass factory.
They stood and watched great ovens
blazing with fire.
The men who blew the glass
stood close to the fires.
Their faces were black
with soot and sweat.

Then Florence saw the children.

Small boys sat by the roaring ovens.

Their job was to run back and forth

carrying loads of newly made bottles.

The bottles were very hot.

The boys looked tired

and dirty and scared.

Florence felt sad

and frightened for them.

Her mother thought that Florence
was too young to see such things.
But her father said that life
could never be right for all children
until people knew about
the lives of the poor.
Florence never forgot her father's words.
She decided she would spend her life
telling as many people as she could
the truth about
the lives of poor children.

When Florence was a child,
she was often sick.
She could not go to school.
But she read many books at home.
And when she was old enough,
she went away to college.
There, she began to study poor children.
She learned all about
the history of working children.

In 1911, in Pittston, Pennsylvania,
a 13-year-old boy named Willie Bryden
worked long hours in a coal mine,
500 feet under the ground.
The mine was dark and cold and damp.
Black coal dust filled the air.
Willie's job was to sit all alone
in a mine shaft, waiting for coal cars.

When he heard a car
coming down the tracks,
he had to stand on the tracks
to open a gate for the car.
If he did not jump off the tracks
soon enough, a car would hit him.
Boys at that time had many jobs
in mines, sometimes working
from seven in the morning
until seven at night.
The money Willie earned would not even
buy his family food for one day.

11

After college, Florence spent time
traveling and studying.

She got married and had three children.

In 1891, when Florence was 32 years old,
she left her husband.

With her children, she moved to Chicago.

Chicago had many factories,

where people made all kinds of things.

They made clothing, candy, books,

bottles, beds, knives,

and everything people needed to live.

Children worked

in some of these factories.

Some were only five years old.

They worked long hours

in dark rooms with dangerous machines.

They didn't make much money.

But they had to work.

Their parents worked.

Many parents couldn't afford

food and clothes for their children

unless the children worked too.

Florence saw all this and was angry.

She decided to fight for the children.

She would fight for laws

that would stop them from working.

It is not easy to change the law.

Florence knew that she had to show

the lawmakers the truth.

She had to show them that many children

were poor and sick and had to work

instead of going to school.

She knew that first

she had to learn the facts.

So Florence set out to learn the truth

about the poor in Chicago.

The best place to find out about
the poor in Chicago in 1891
was at a place called Hull-House.
A group of women lived and worked there,
led by a woman named Jane Addams.
These women worked together
to try to solve the city's worst problems.

Jane welcomed Florence
and put her to work right away.
The government wanted
to study poor people
in the largest American cities.
Jane asked Florence to write a report
about the slums of Chicago.

At that time, not many people
paid attention to the poor.
Florence could not find the facts
she needed in books.
She had to find them out herself.
Florence and her workers went into
the poorest parts of the city.
They knocked on doors
and talked to the people there.
They asked many questions.
They asked how many children lived there,
and how much money the parents earned.
They asked whether the children worked
or went to school.
They wrote down all of
these facts and numbers.
When they had gone to hundreds of houses,
Florence added up all of the facts.

Bertie Batsen was 10 years old in 1908,
and she had already worked for 3 years
in a mill that made cloth
in Dillon, South Carolina.
The little girl walked up and down
the long rows of spinning machines,
finding broken threads and mending them.
Bertie worked 10 to 12 hours a day,
6 days a week.

Much of what Florence learned upset her.
She saw that many children under 14
were working and not going to school.
She saw that both adults and children
had to work in very bad conditions.
Often the workplaces were noisy.
Some were very dirty,
and some had no windows
to let in light and fresh air.
There were many dangerous machines.
Some workers had bad accidents.
If they lost an arm or a leg,
they had to stop working.

Florence wrote a report
that was filled with exact numbers.
She added many sad stories
about the people she had met.
Florence gave her report
to the lawmakers.
But she did not stop there.

She began to make speeches
wherever she could.
She spoke out at churches
and meetings and clubs.
She even took groups of people
into the poor parts of the city
so they could see for themselves
how the poor lived and worked.

When Florence Kelley spoke,
people paid attention.
She was a large woman,
with dark eyes
and lots of beautiful brown hair.
She always dressed
in plain black clothing,
and when she was angry,
she could look rather frightening.
Her smooth, deep voice
was sometimes very quiet,
but could rise to a powerful boom.
Florence chose her words carefully
and was able to think quickly.
Even her enemies listened to her.

In 1893, after they had read
Florence's reports,
Illinois lawmakers made a law
that stopped people from working
more than eight hours a day.
This law also stopped children
under the age of 14
from working at all.
The new law said that someone
had to visit the factories
to make sure that the owners
followed the law.

So the governor made Florence
the first Chief Factory Inspector
in Illinois.
One of the first things
Florence tried to do
was to stop a factory
from hiring small children.
The children were painting picture frames
with paint that had poison in it.
Breathing near the paint
made the children sick.

Florence went to a lawyer,
and asked him to sue the factory.
But he said no,
that he had more important things to do.
Florence realized that she could not
depend on lawyers to help her.
So she went to law school
to learn how to fight
her own battles in court.

In those days,

very few women went to college

and even fewer went to law school.

But Florence did not let that stop her.

A few years later,

she received her law degree.

To make laws and change laws,

a person must understand them.

Learning about the law

was useful to Florence

all the rest of her life.

In Bay St. Louis, Mississippi, in 1911,
many small children worked
in a canning factory.
Some were as young as three years old.
They helped their families
take the shells off shrimp.
The shrimp were kept on ice.
On cold days, fingers would get stiff.

Children cut their fingers
on the sharp shells, and the juices
from the shrimp burned terribly.
At some canneries, families had
only small, dirty shacks to live in.
There were no lights or toilets.
A family was paid for
the number of shrimp they peeled.
They had to work long and fast
to earn enough money to live.

As Chief Factory Inspector,
Florence wrote about all that she saw.
Sometimes there was danger.
Once she found out that some workers
were very sick with smallpox,
a serious disease.
The clothes they were making
had smallpox germs on them.

Florence knew that people
who bought the clothes
could get sick and die.
If she went into the building,
she could catch smallpox herself.
But she bravely went in
and made the owners close the factory.

Sometimes factory bosses
were angry with Florence.
It cost them less money to hire children
than to pay adult workers.
They did not want to follow the new laws.
Once someone even fired a gun
to stop Florence
from going into a building.
But she could not be stopped.
For four years, she did her best
to make sure
that factory owners followed the law.

Florence found other ways
to help the poor.
She thought that everyone should know
about the way the owners
of some factories treated their workers.
She thought that if people knew
how these workers were treated,
they wouldn't want to buy the things
that these factories made.
They would stop buying them
until the owners changed the way
they treated the workers.

Many people agreed with Florence.
They formed groups across the country
to let people know
about companies that used child workers
or treated their adult workers badly.
These groups were called
Consumers Leagues, because consumers
are people who buy things.
Florence joined
the Consumers League in Illinois.

In 1898, Florence moved to New York
to become the leader
of the National Consumers League.
She traveled all over the country,
giving speeches and telling people
about the work of the League.
She spoke out to say
that workers should be paid more.
She called for shorter work hours
and the end of child labor.
Many of the people who listened
became upset and angry.
Many voted for lawmakers who
they hoped would change things.

Many children worked in their homes.

Factories often gave people work

to finish at home.

Women and children

would spend hours every day

making silk flowers

or sewing buttons on shirts.

Even tiny children could help.

Some children sat sewing in poor light

from the time they got home from school

until late at night.

They were so tired,

they often fell asleep at school.

In 1908, in a house on Sullivan Street
in New York, three children
worked with their mother to make
about 1,600 silk flowers a day.
For this, they earned
barely enough to buy food.

Another way Florence fought for children
was by helping to start
the United States Children's Bureau.
She wanted to know
facts about all children in the United States,
and she believed that
only a big national office
could collect these facts.
The first job of the Children's Bureau
was to learn why
so many American children died
while they were still babies.
No one knew exactly how many
babies died each year.

When the bureau counted
the deaths of babies
for the whole United States in one year,
the number was 250,000.
This number was larger
than anyone had thought.
The Children's Bureau report said
that new mothers
needed better health care.
Congress agreed to give money
for health care
to poor mothers and their children.

When Florence Kelley died in 1932,
her work was not yet done.
Some of the laws she had helped to make
had later been changed or cancelled.
Twice, the U.S. Congress
had voted for laws that stopped children
under the age of 14 from working.
But both times the Supreme Court
had not allowed the new laws to pass.

In the end, however,
it was not so important
that Florence Kelley lost
a few of her battles.
In later years, others found ways
to get the needed laws,
often by doing just as Florence had done:
They made sure
that people knew the facts.

"Beet-topping" was a job for children
in the fields near Sterling, Colorado,
in 1915.
For 12 hours a day, boys and girls
used huge, hooked knives
to cut the tops from the beet plants.

Families who did this kind of work
often moved from one farm to another
to find enough work.
They never earned enough money
to buy homes of their own.
They worked in all weather,
rain or shine, bending over all day long.

We have laws
that keep children from working.
We have laws that give all children
the right to go to school.
And we have laws that help protect
workers from danger and sickness.
In this way, Florence succeeded.

But in some places,

children still work hard.

They work long hours,

in dangerous places.

They do not go to school.

Florence Kelley did all she could

to stop these things from happening.

With the lessons learned from her,

others will keep trying

to make things right for all children.

Important Dates

1859—Florence Kelley is born in Philadelphia. (Her exact date of birth is uncertain.)

1859-1876—Grows up in Philadelphia, attending Quaker schools when healthy

1876—Enters Cornell University in Ithaca, New York

1883-1886—Studies at the University of Zurich in Switzerland

1886—Returns to the United States and lives in New York

1891— Moves to Chicago and goes to live at Hull-House

1893—Becomes first Chief Inspector of Factories for Illinois

1895—Receives law degree from Northwestern University in Evanston, Illinois

1899—Moves to New York to lead the National Consumers League

1906-1912—Helps to create the United States Children's Bureau

1932—Died in New York City